Kid's Box

New Generation

British English

Caroline Nixon &
Michael Tomlinson

CAMBRIDGE

Pupil's Book
with eBook

4

Language summary

	Key vocabulary	Key language	Sounds and spelling
 **Hello there!** page 4	Character names Adjectives for personal descriptions **Daily routines:** *clean your teeth, comb your hair, eat your breakfast, get dressed, get up, get your bag, have a wash, put on your shoes, wake up* **Jobs:** *detective, doctor, driver, farmer*	Comparative adjectives **Adverbs of frequency:** *always, sometimes, never* *have to, like/love + -ing, want to be*	*ur – curly* *ir – girl* *ay – play* **The long *i* sound:** *night, ride*
1 Back to school page 10	**Adjectives:** *boring, busy, careful, difficult, easy, exciting, quick, slow, terrible*	Relative clauses with *who*	**Stressed syllables:** *ex<u>ci</u>ting* *<u>bor</u>ing*

Art: How can we use paint?   page 16

	Key vocabulary	Key language	Sounds and spelling
2 Good sports page 18	*inside, outside* **Activities:** *climb, dance, fish, ice skate, roller skate, sail, skateboard, swim*	*learn (how) to (do something)* Relative clauses with *where* Adverbs of manner	**Consonant clusters:** *sk – skate* *sl – sloth* *sp – sports* *sw – swing*

Sport: What urban sports can we do?   page 24

Review: units 1 and 2   page 26

	Key vocabulary	Key language	Sounds and spelling
3 Health matters page 28	**Health:** *dentist, have a dream, have an eye test, hospital, ill, nurse, see the doctor, take some medicine*	**Past simple irregular verbs:** affirmative, negative, interrogative and short answers Clauses with *because*	*b – burger* *v – vegetables*

Career-related learning: What makes a job fun?   page 34

	Key vocabulary	Key language	Sounds and spelling
4 After school club page 36	**Activities:** *do a musical, play chess / table tennis* **Ordinal numbers:** *first to twentieth*	**Past simple regular verbs:** affirmative, negative, interrogative and short answers	*-ed* endings

Maths: What can a survey tell us?   page 42

Review: units 3 and 4   page 44

	Key vocabulary	Key language	Sounds and spelling
5 Exploring our world page 46	**Exploring:** *Antarctica, continents, exhibition, expedition, explorer, ice, make a camp, museum, school trip, ship*	Past simple irregular verbs Clauses with *so* Comparative adjectives and adverbs	*ir – circus* *ur – purple* *or – world*
Geography: How can I stay safe outdoors? page 52			
6 Technology page 54	**Technology:** *app, button, DVD, email, the internet, keyboard, laptop, mobile phone, mouse, screen, text message, turn on, video*	Past simple irregular verbs	*ou – brought* *or – sports* *a – talk*
Technology: How does technology help us? page 60			
Review: units 5 and 6 page 62			
7 At the zoo page 64	**Animals:** *bear, bird, blue whale, crocodile, dolphin, elephant, giraffe, kangaroo, lion, lizard, monkey, panda, parrot, rabbit, shark, tiger*	Superlative adjectives Past simple irregular and regular verbs **Prepositions:** *along, around/round, into, out of*	*ew – flew* *ue – blue* *oo – zoo* *oo – wood*
Science: How are life cycles different? page 70			
8 Let's party! page 72	**Containers:** *bottle, bowl, box, cup, glass* **Food:** *cheese, pasta, salad, sandwich, soup, vegetables*	**Expressions of quantity:** *a bottle/bowl/box/cup/glass of* *want someone to (do something)* Superlative adverbs Past simple irregular and regular verbs	Review
Literature: How can we write poetry? page 78			
Review: units 7 and 8 page 80			

Hello there!

 🎧 2 **Look, think and answer. Listen and check.**

1 What does Stella want to be?
2 Who's a farmer?
3 What's Simon reading?
4 Who's riding Suzy's bike?

 Listen again. Choose the right words.

1 Stella's **twelve** / **twenty** / **ten**.
2 Simon's older than **Suzy** / **Stella** / **May**.
3 Fred is Simon's **father** / **brother** / **uncle**.
4 Simon wants to be a **farmer** / **detective** / **dentist**.
5 Aunt May's **younger** / **older** / **smaller** than Suzy.

> Stella's ten.

 Talk about your family.

> My dad is older than my mum.

LOOK

Stella's **older than** Simon.
Simon's **younger than** Stella.

4   Language: revision

1 Read and match.

1 – h

1 His hair is grey and curly. He's funny.
2 He's got short black hair and he's wearing sunglasses. He's hungry.
3 She's got straight grey hair. She's thirsty.
4 She's got short brown hair and she's young. She's little, but loud.
5 She's got blonde hair and she isn't young. She's quiet.
6 He's got short straight red hair. He's happy.
7 She's got straight blonde hair and she wears glasses. She's clever.
8 He's got blonde hair, a beard and a moustache. He smiles a lot.
9 She's got straight black hair. She's tired.

2  3 Listen and say the name.

> 1 Who smiles a lot?   Uncle Fred.

3 Play the game.

> Has he got blonde hair?   Is he younger than Stella?   Is he Uncle Fred?

> Yes, he has.   No, he isn't.   Yes, he is.

Vocabulary: adjectives for personal descriptions   5

Read the information and answer.

1 Where does Aunt May work?
2 What does she like doing?

3 Where does Uncle Fred live?
4 What time does he get up?

Aunt May's a doctor. She works in a big hospital in the city. She sometimes works during the day and she sometimes has to work at night. She doesn't like working at the weekend. She likes listening to music and taking photos.

Uncle Fred's a farmer. He lives on a farm in the country. He's got twenty-seven cows and forty-three sheep. He always gets up at five o'clock. Uncle Fred has to work in the morning, the afternoon and the evening. He sometimes works at night too. He loves working on his farm and driving his lorry!

 Correct the sentences.

Aunt May's a doctor.

1 Aunt May's a bus driver.
2 She works in a big school.
3 She never works at night.
4 She likes working at the weekend.

5 Uncle Fred lives in a flat in the city.
6 He's got forty-three cows.
7 He never gets up at five o'clock.
8 He always works at night.

STUDY

She **always** wears a white coat at work.

He **sometimes** works at night.

He **never** gets up at ten o'clock.

Language: adverbs of frequency

1 ♫ ∩ 4 ▶ Read the song and order the pictures. Listen and check.

The morning rap,
We do it every day.
The same routine,
Now listen and say.

It's seven o'clock,
Wake up, wake up!
You must get up
And have a wash.

Come on, come on,
It's time to go.
Get dressed, get dressed!
Put on your clothes.

Run to the kitchen,
Sit on a chair.
Eat your breakfast,
Comb your hair.

The morning rap ...

It's seven o'clock ...

Clean your teeth.
No time to lose.
Get your bag,
Put on your shoes.

Goodbye to Mum,
Goodbye to Dad.
My friends are at school,
So I'm not sad.

The morning rap.
The morning rap.

2 ♫ ∩ 5 ▶ Sing the song. Do karaoke.

3 Write about your day.

I wake up at seven o'clock.
I get dressed after I get up ...

Vocabulary: daily routines   **7**

 **Lock's sounds and spelling**

1 🎵 🎧 6 ▶ **Watch the video. Watch again and practise.**

2 **Write the words in the correct box. Say.**

The girl with curly hair plays all day.

She rides a bike all night.

_____ rides _____

_____ girl _____

_____ plays _____

3 **Choose and say to make sentences.**

The farmer …

The farmer always …

The farmer always wakes up early …

The farmer always wakes up early in the morning!

girl with curly hair farmer dentist detective builder nurse	always sometimes never	wakes up early takes a train rides a bike flies a kite	all day all night in the morning in the afternoon in the evening

Show what you know

c _____ ly   g _____ l

Sounds and spelling: *-ur, -ir, -ay, -i* and *-igh* spellings

1 Look at the pictures. Describe what's happening.

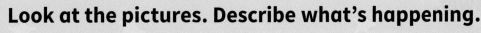

In picture 1, Mrs Potts asks Lock and Key for help.

1 Back to school

1 🎧 8 **Look, think and answer. Listen and check.**

1 Where are the children?

2 Which class are Simon and Alex in?

3 Who likes Maths?

4 What's Meera doing?

2 🎧 9 **Listen and match.**

1 careful   2 boring   3 difficult   4 exciting   5 slow
6 easy   7 busy   8 quick   9 terrible

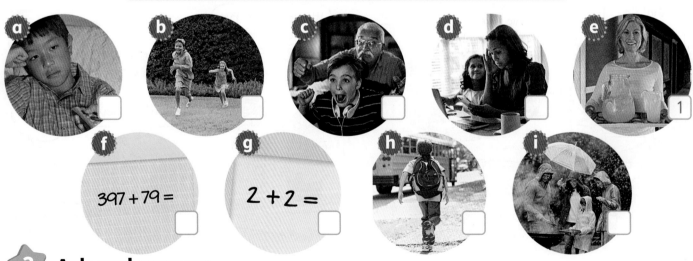

3 **Ask and answer.**

What do you like at school?   I like Sport because it's exciting.

Read and say the names.

Daisy

Jordan

Yasmin

Johnny

Zak

1 This child likes being busy with lots of homework.
His hair is straight and black and he's got glasses. — Johnny

2 This child loves Art and is careful at painting.
He's got short curly brown hair.

3 The child with straight blonde hair is very brave.
She loves reading to her class.

4 This child with glasses thinks Maths is exciting.
Her hair is brown and curly.

5 This child with short straight blonde hair thinks Music is difficult.

 Make sentences and say 'true' or 'false'.

The child with curly hair and glasses thinks Maths is boring. — False.

 Read and correct the text.

My teacher
This is Mr Harrison. He's my Maths teacher.
He works in a school in a big city. He's very sbyu
because he's got a lot of work. There are 28
children in my class. His lessons aren't wols or
grinbo, they're very ecgitxin. We like his lessons
because they're not ftlcuidfi. It's yase to learn
lots of new things with him. Mr Harrison is very
fclareu when he writes, but I'm not!

 Write about one of your teachers.

Look, think and answer. Listen and check.

1 Where are the Star family?
2 Who's Mrs Star talking to?

3 Who's the Music teacher?
4 Who's the Art teacher?

Play the game.

He's the teacher who's talking to Mrs Star.   Mr Newton.

STUDY

She's the woman **who's** wearing the long green skirt.
He's the man **who's** carrying the lorry.

Language: relative clauses with *who*

1 Read and match.

1 – d

1 They're the boys who are laughing.
2 She's the girl who's drinking orange juice.
3 He's the boy who's wearing a red sweater.
4 They're the girls who are wearing blue dresses.
5 She's the girl who's skipping.
6 He's the boy who's throwing a ball.

2 Choose a child. Ask and answer.

Is it the boy who's reading a comic?

No, it isn't.

3 🎵🎧 11 ▶ Read and say the letter. Listen and check.

The classroom's where you learn,
The classroom's where we teach,
Lots of exciting things,
To do in our school week.

1 I teach Sport,
It's quick, not slow,
Run, jump and skip,
Go, go, go!

2 I teach English,
All I need,
Are lots of words,
And books to read.

3 I teach Maths,
It's easy to add,
But if it's wrong,
Don't be sad.

4 I teach Art,
We can paint and draw,
Careful with the paint,
Don't drop it on the floor!

The classroom's where you learn,
The classroom's where we teach,
Lots of exciting things,
To do in our school week.

4 🎵🎧 12 ▶ Sing the song. Do karaoke.

Lock's sounds and spelling

1 🎧 13 ▶ **Watch the video. Watch again and practise.**

2 **Circle the stressed syllables. Say.**

THE JUNGLE SCHOOL

$8+5=$
$17-6=$

Art is **ea**sy for elephant, but difficult for snake.

Maths is exciting for snake, but boring for elephant.

In Sport, snake is quick, but elephant is slow.

3 **Say and guess.**

> He's doing Maths and it's difficult.

> The elephant?

THE JUNGLE SCHOOL

FINISH

$12598 \times 5/8$

Show what you know

difficult   slow   easy   exciting   quick   boring   amazing

●	●○	●○○	○●○
		difficult	

What do Lock and Key do at Peter's school? Say three things.

How can we use paint?

1 🎧 15 **Listen and read. Which artist's style was new?**

The Couple is a painting by Georges Seurat, a French artist. He invented a style of painting called 'pointillism'. The artist uses small dots and dashes of colour to paint a picture. You need to look at the painting from far away to see the image clearly.

I like the painting because it makes me feel relaxed. It reminds me of a warm, summer morning.

The Frame is a painting by Frida Kahlo. She was a famous artist from Mexico. She liked to paint 'self-portraits' – paintings of herself. Frida looks confident in the painting. She's got beautiful flowers in her hair. There are also bright colourful flowers and birds around her. They are traditional images from old Mexican stories.

The painting makes me curious about Frida Kahlo and her life in Mexico. I want to learn more about her!

2 **Read again and complete the notes for Frida Kahlo.**

Artist:	Georges Seurat	Frida Kahlo
Painting:	The Couple	
Style:	pointillism	
Description:	a painting that uses dots and dashes	
Feeling:	relaxed	

3 **Which painting do you prefer? Why?**

DIDYOUKNOW...?
In 'drip' artwork, artists drip paint instead of using a paintbrush.

1

4 **Read the description. What do you see when you look at this painting?**

A description of 'Composition in blue, red and yellow'

This painting is by a Dutch artist called Piet Mondrian. It is 'abstract' art. It doesn't show people or objects. It uses lines, shapes and bright colours to make a picture. In this painting, the artist uses thick black lines to make squares and rectangles. It reminds me of a big colourful window.

Some of the shapes are painted blue, red and yellow. They are my favourite colours because they make me feel calm and peaceful.

by Samir Ali

5 **Underline the descriptive adjectives in Activity 4.**

Ready to write:

Go to Activity Book page 16.

Learning to write:

Descriptive adjectives

There are also **bright colourful** flowers and birds around her.

6 **Ask and answer about the painting. Complete the table.**

Do you like the painting? Why or why not?	
What does it remind you of?	
How does it make you feel?	
What is an example of a painting or a style of painting you like? Why?	

Project

Make a classroom gallery.

2 Good sports

ACTIVITIES OUTSIDE

fish

swim

skateboard

sail

roller skate

ACTIVITIES INSIDE

dance

ice skate

climb

1 🎧 16 Look, think and answer. Listen and check.

1 Who do you think wants to climb?

2 How many water sports can they do?

3 Where can they do water sports?

4 Which activity can they do inside and outside?

2 🎧 17 Listen and say the letter.

1 He's at the ice rink. He's learning how to ice skate.

h

a

b

c

d

e

f

g

h

3 Ask and answer.

Which activities do you want to do?

I want to dance.

Read and tick (✓) for you. Ask three friends and answer.

> Do you want to learn to skateboard?

> Yes, I do.

What do you want to learn to do?						
Name	skateboard	dance	climb	sail	ice skate	fish
Me	☐	☐	☐	☐	☐	☐
___	☐	☐	☐	☐	☐	☐
___	☐	☐	☐	☐	☐	☐
___	☐	☐	☐	☐	☐	☐

 Write a report.

STUDY

I	want to	learn to	sail.
My teacher	wants to doesn't want to	learn to learn how to	dance. climb. ice skate.
My friends	want to don't want to		skip.

___ In my class, Daisy and Hugo want to learn how to skateboard, but
Jack doesn't want to learn to skateboard. He wants to learn to dance.

 Read and write the words.

> park   lake   ice rink   road   ~~skate park~~

1 A place where you can learn how to roller skate.   skate park
2 A place where you can go ice skating.   ___
3 A place where you can learn to ride a bike.   ___
4 A place where you can learn how to sail.   ___
5 A place where you mustn't skateboard.   ___

 Ask and answer to guess the place.

> Is it a place where you can learn how to sail?

> Yes.

> A lake!

 **1** 🎧 18 ▶ **Look, think and answer. Listen and check.**

1 Where's Mr Star?

2 Who's climbing?

3 Where's Grandpa Star?

4 What's Suzy doing?

badly   carefully   quickly   slowly   well

 2 **Read and choose the right words.**

1 They're running **quietly** / **quickly** / **slowly**.

2 They're shouting **loudly** / **quietly** / **carefully**.

3 He's playing **badly** / **loudly** / **well**.

4 They're reading **quietly** / **loudly** / **badly**.

5 They're running **quickly** / **well** / **slowly**.

6 She's playing **well** / **loudly** / **badly**.

7 He's riding his bike **carefully** / **loudly** / **quickly**.

quickly

 3 **Play the game.**   Find the children who are reading quietly.   Number 4.

Language: adverbs of manner

1  🎧 **19** **Listen and say 'yes' or 'no'.**

> **1** They're playing well.   Yes.

2 🎵🎧 **20** ▶ **Complete. Listen and check.**

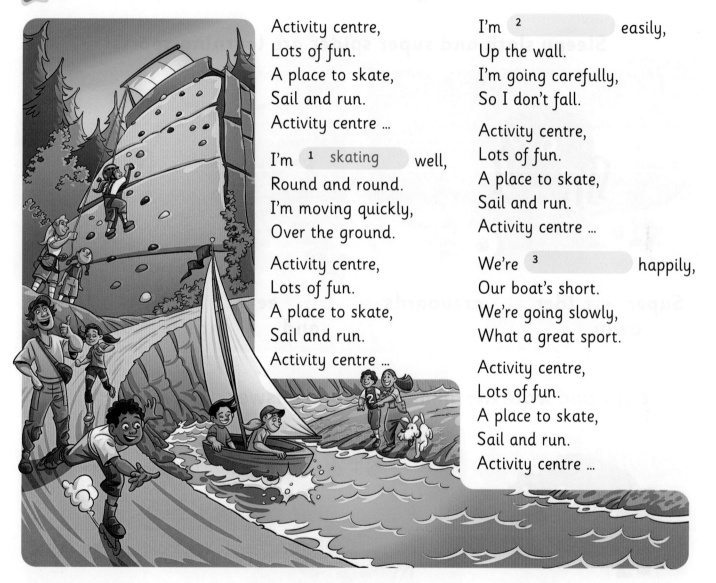

Activity centre,
Lots of fun.
A place to skate,
Sail and run.
Activity centre …

I'm **1** skating well,
Round and round.
I'm moving quickly,
Over the ground.

Activity centre,
Lots of fun.
A place to skate,
Sail and run.
Activity centre …

I'm **2** _____ easily,
Up the wall.
I'm going carefully,
So I don't fall.

Activity centre,
Lots of fun.
A place to skate,
Sail and run.
Activity centre …

We're **3** _____ happily,
Our boat's short.
We're going slowly,
What a great sport.

Activity centre,
Lots of fun.
A place to skate,
Sail and run.
Activity centre …

3  🎵🎧 **21** ▶ **Sing the song. Do karaoke.**

4 **Write another verse. Sing.**

I'm **running** / **dancing** / **skipping** well,
Look at me.
Doing it **slowly** / **quickly** / **happily**,
Can you see?

I'm dancing well,
Look at me.

Lock's sounds and spelling

1 🎧 22 ▶ **Watch the video. Watch again and practise.**

2 **Read and complete. Say.**

Sleepy sloth and super spider are learning sports!

Super _s__p_ ider _____ ateboards _____ owly.

_____ eepy _____ oth _____ ims and _____ ings _____ owly.

3 **Look and write the animal. Ask and answer.**

Can you skateboard like a sloth?

Yes, look!

No, I can't.

| skateboard | swim | swing | do sports | ice skate | roller skate |

Show what you know

I can't _____ im, but I can _____ ateboard!

Sounds and spelling: consonant clusters: *sk, sl, sp, sw*

Lock & Key!

1 **Act out the story. What's your favourite part?**

▶ What urban sports can we do?

1 🎧 24 **Listen and read. What is important for both sports?**

URBAN SPORTS

SKATEBOARDING

Skateboarding is a popular sport here in Barcelona. To start, you need a skateboard.

You stand carefully on the board to ride it. When people skateboard, they do tricks. They jump and turn quickly.

The best thing about skateboarding is that you can do it anywhere. There are special skate parks here, but a lot of people skateboard on the street.

HOCKEY

Canada is famous for the sport hockey. The players play in teams and move a small disc (called a 'puck') with a long stick. They try to hit the puck into a goal. You have to score goals to win.

We have hockey fields here, but kids also play it on the street and you can play it wearing skates.

SAFETY

 ⚠ Wear a helmet so you don't hurt yourself badly if you fall.

⚠ Don't do sport near busy roads.

2 **Read again and complete. Talk to a friend about another sport you can do in the street.**

What's similar?	What's different?
You mustn't do it near busy roads.	Skateboarding uses a board and hockey uses a stick.

3 **Which sport would you like to do? Why?**

DIDYOUKNOW...?
Skateboarding started in California. The idea was to make a surfboard with wheels for the street!

4 Read the poster. Write the headings.

How to play   Players   ~~Get ready~~   How to win!

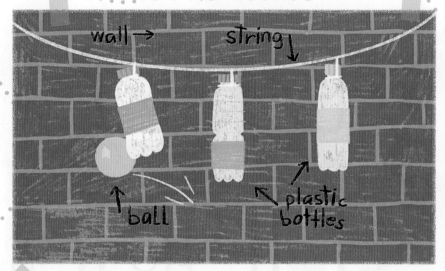

Get ready

Bottle Bounce is a fun game you can play almost anywhere. You just need string, a ball and some plastic bottles. Tie the bottles carefully to a string and hang them near a wall, like the picture.

wall →   string ↓

ball ↑   plastic bottles ↖

Players throw the ball directly at the wall. The ball bounces quickly off the wall and hits the bottles. It's a fun game, but it's difficult to play well.

The player who hits the most bottles wins.

You can play Bottle Bounce with 2-4 players. All you need is enough space and enough bottles!

5 Circle the adverbs in Activity 4.

Ready to write:

Go to Activity Book page 24.

Learning to write:
Adverbs
They jump and turn **quickly**.
Wear a helmet so you don't hurt yourself **badly** if you fall.

6 Read again and complete. Why is *Bottle Bounce* a good urban sport?

1 Between ___2___ and _____ players can play *Bottle Bounce*.
2 Players use a _____ to hit some _____.
3 The ball has to _____ off the wall before it hits the _____.
4 You can _____ *Bottle Bounce* almost _____.

Project

Make a presentation about a sport in a different country.

Sport: What urban sports can we do?   collaboration   25

Review Units 1 and 2

1 **Play the game.**

⭐2 Read the text and choose the best answer.

Example

Tony: Hi, Sue. What are you doing?

Sue: (A) I'm playing badminton.
   B I'm playing baseball.
   C I'm hitting the ball.

Questions

1 **Tony:** Who are you playing with?
   Sue: A She's my Aunt Sue.
   B My brother, Alex.
   C We're playing well.

2 **Tony:** Is he older than you?
   Sue: A No, he's my brother.
   B Yes, he's holding the ball.
   C No, he's a year younger than me.

3 **Tony:** Are you good at badminton?
   Sue: A Yes, I've got three.
   B I'm not bad, but Alex is better than me.
   C No, thank you.

4 **Sue:** Do you like badminton?
   Tony: A Yes, it's my favourite sport.
   B Yes, please.
   C Yes, let's.

5 **Sue:** Would you like to play badminton with us?
   Tony: A I'd like that, thanks.
   B Yes, I like board games.
   C No, I don't.

6 **Sue:** Shall I start?
   Tony: A Yes, I want to stop.
   B No, I want to play.
   C Yes, good idea.

1 What does Simon want to be? (p4)

2 Which child loves Art and is careful at painting? (p11)

3 Where were Lock and Key on Thursday morning? (p15)

4 Name a painting by Frida Kahlo. (p16)

5 What's Suzy learning to do? (p20)

6 Name a place where you can learn to climb and sail. (p21)

7 Why does Key go and see Mr Sweep? (p23)

8 Which sport uses a puck? (p24)

3 Health matters

was   were   had   drank   saw   gave   took   went   ate

1 🎧 25 **Look, think and answer. Listen and check.**

1 What was Simon's temperature?   3 Why were Simon and his mum at the hospital?
2 Where was Simon on Thursday?   4 When was Simon well again?

2 🎧 26 **Listen and say the day.**

> 1 The doctor gave him some medicine.   Wednesday.

3 **Talk about the last time you were ill.**

> Last time I was ill, I drank orange juice because I had a cold.

Language: past simple irregular verbs

Read and match.

1   He took some medicine because he had a cold.
2   We ate a lot because we were hungry.
3   She went to bed early because she was ill.
4   I drank a lot because I had a temperature.
5   The doctor gave her some medicine because she had a stomach-ache.
6   They saw the dentist because they had a toothache.

| d |
| |
| |
| |
| |
| |

 Read and answer the questions.

Last Monday morning, Sue went to the City Hospital to see the doctor because she had a headache. When she was at the hospital, the doctor gave her an eye test. After her eye test, Sue saw her friend Tom. He was at the hospital because he was ill. He was happy to see Sue. The nurse gave him some medicine. Then he had lunch in bed and he drank orange juice. At one o'clock, Sue was hungry so she went home.

1   Why was Sue at the hospital?   Because she had a headache.
2   Who had an eye test?
3   Which of Sue's friends was at the hospital?
4   Why was Tom happy?
5   Who gave Tom some medicine?
6   Where was Tom when he had lunch?
7   Who drank orange juice?
8   What time was it when Sue went home?

STUDY

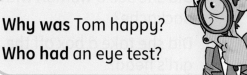

Why was Tom happy?
Who had an eye test?

1 🎧 27 ▶ Look, think and answer. Listen and check.

1 Who's Stella talking to this morning?
2 Where was Stella in her dream?

3 What was Stella's job?
4 What was wrong with the man?

This morning

Last night

2 Read and answer.

1 Did Stella have a nice dream?
2 Did she have a long blue coat?
3 Did she see a woman who had a cough?
4 Did she give the man some flowers?
5 Did she see a woman with backache?
6 Did she take a box off the girl's head?

No, she didn't. She had a terrible dream.

STUDY

have ➔ had   do ➔ did
I **had** a terrible dream.
I **didn't have** time to stop.
How many people **did** you **see**?
Did she **give** the man some flowers?
Yes, she **did.** / No, she **didn't.**

Language: past simple irregular verbs: negative, interrogative and short answers

 Read and say the word. Listen and check.

lemonade   ice cream   burgers   chocolate   three
water   party   sausages   ~~nurse~~   fruit

Mummy, Mummy, call the ! [nurse]
I had a stomach-ache but now
it's worse.

What's the matter?

I don't know,
But please be quick,
Don't be slow.

Did you have a  yesterday?

Yes! There was lots to eat and
games to play.

Did you eat ?

Yes, I did.

Did you eat ?

Yes, I did.

Did you drink ?

Yes, I did.

Did you have and too?
I think I know what's the matter
with you!
Take this medicine **3** times a day,
When you are better, go out and play!

No more chocolate cake for you,
my daughter.
Vegetables, and a drink of !

2 🎵🎧 29 ▶ Sing the song. Do karaoke.

3 Ask and answer about the song.

[Did she eat ice cream?]   [Yes, she did.]

[Did she drink orange juice?]   [No, she didn't.]

Lock's sounds and spelling

 1 🎧 30 ▶ **Watch the video. Watch again and practise.**

2 **Circle the letter 'b' and underline the letter 'v'. Say.**

A (b)ig bear had a <u>v</u>ery bad backache and went to see the vet.

'Vegetables and rest are best,' said the vet.

 3 **Write sentences. Say and guess.**

There's a boy …

… in the living room with a very big ball!

No, sorry. Try again!

a bear		a very big ball
a boy	bathroom	a burger
a bird	kitchen	some vegetables
a vet	bedroom	some breakfast
a bat	living room	a TV

Show what you know

When I'm hungry, I like to eat ___egetables and ___urgers.

Sounds and spelling: words with *b* and *v*

 31 ▶

1 **Who did Key see in the hospital shop? Describe the man.**

Story: unit language in context   33

▶ What makes a job fun?

1 🎧 **32** **Listen and read. Which job do you prefer? Why?**

DREAM JOBS

miguel@vidblog.com

I studied Design at college, and now I'm a video game designer. I love playing video games so it's the perfect job for me. I design the characters – they're a lot of fun to create. But the best part of my job is testing the new games.

tania@dancehall.blog

I'm a dancer in pop music videos. I studied ballet, but I like dancing to all kinds of music, from classical to pop and rock. I work with a team of dancers. We practise and perform the dances together. It's fun, but we're always tired after work. You need to be fit to do my job.

steffi@race.com

I'm a racing car driver. I race in competitions all over the world. It can be dangerous, but it's very exciting! You need to be brave to do this job. I don't feel scared when I drive because I trained for many years. When I'm driving, I feel free! I love my job and I love my car.

2 **Read and write 'designer', 'dancer' or 'driver'.**

1 You can work and play at the same time.   designer
2 It's a dangerous job.   _____
3 You need to be fit and healthy.   _____
4 You have to travel to different countries.   _____
5 You mustn't be scared at work.   _____
6 You need to use your imagination.   _____

3 **What makes each job fun?**

┌─ **DIDYOUKNOW...?** ─────────
Truck driver is one of the most popular jobs in the United States. There are more than 3.5 million truck drivers in the country.

4 **Read the blog. Say what Joaquín thinks is fun about his dream job.**

www.myblog.com

My dream job!

My dream job is a professional musician. I took drum lessons last year. Now I'm a drummer in a band and I sing, too. We're all friends in my band so it's fun when we play together. It's an exciting feeling! I want to play shows all over the world one day. Travelling can be tiring, but I'd love to visit lots of different countries. It sounds like so much fun!

joaquin@drumspot.blog

5 **Underline the contractions in Activity 4.**

Ready to write:

Go to Activity Book page 34.

Learning to write:

Contractions
I'm a video game designer.

6 **Read and tick (✓) the correct options. Tell a friend about your dream job.**

Joaquín **is** ☐ **wants to be** ✓ a professional musician.
He studied **drums** ☐ **singing** ☐ .
He thinks playing music with his friends is **exciting** ☐ **hard work** ☐ .
He **travels** ☐ **wants to travel** ☐ all over the world.

Project

Role-play an interview.

4 After school club

1 🎧 33 **Look, think and answer. Listen and check.**

1 Where did the children go yesterday afternoon?

2 Which teacher was there?

3 Who did Stella play chess with?

4 Who wasn't good at dancing?

2 🎧 34 **Listen and say 'yes' or 'no'.**

1 The children helped Mr Star.   No.

3 **What did you do after school yesterday? Write.**

I went to the library because I wanted to get a book.

1 Read and match.

a Pat worked at a school. She was the cook. She cooked all the food in the morning. The children liked eating her pancakes! After school, she helped the children as they skipped, jumped and danced in the playground. ☐

b Tod lived in the countryside. He loved sport, and he climbed and sailed every weekend. When it rained, he called his friend, Fred. Tod and Fred went to the After school club, where they played badminton inside. ☐

c Yesterday, David chatted with his friend Sid and invited him to go ice skating. It was very cold so they needed hats and scarves. It started to snow, but Sid ice skated on the lake. David pointed and shouted because Sid wasn't careful. ☐

2 🎧 35 Listen and say 'a', 'b' or 'c'.

1 It started to snow.   c

3 Read and answer.

1 Where did Pat work?   *She worked at a school.*
2 What did Pat cook?
3 When did Pat help the children?
4 Where did Tod live?
5 What did Tod do every weekend?

6 What did Tod and Fred play inside?
7 Who did David chat with?
8 What did they need?
9 Where did Sid skate?

 **36 ▶ Look, think and answer. Listen and check.**

1 Which friend are the children visiting?
3 Who loves climbing?
2 Where is Alex's flat?
4 Why must they walk up the stairs?

 Read and answer.

1 What's the third letter of the alphabet? C
2 What's the ninth letter?
3 What's the twelfth letter?
4 What's the sixteenth letter?
5 What's the twentieth letter?

 Write more questions to ask a friend.

LOOK	
first	1st
second	2nd
third	3rd
fourth	4th
fifth	5th

Vocabulary: ordinal numbers: *first* to *twentieth*

Listen and complete. Sing the song. Do karaoke.

SCHOOL DANCE

Dancing is good, dancing is fine,
Dancing is great!
Come on, children! Dance in line!

First, ^a second , third and fourth,
Dance, dance across the floor.
^b , sixth, seventh, ^c ,
Jump, kick, don't come in late.
^d , tenth, eleventh, ^e ,
Dancing is ^f for your health.

Dancing's good, dancing's fine,
Come on, children! Dance in line!

Number five's ^g ,
And number ten's last.
He can't hop and skip,
He can't get past.

Dancing is good, dancing is fine,
Dancing is great!
Come on, children! Dance in line!

 Ask and answer.

Which team was twentieth last week?

The Goal Monsters.

Last Week
1. Heart Club 8. Great Movers 15. Dirty Players
2. All Sports 9. Dream Team   16. Walking Legs
                                17. The Terrible Tigers
This Week   18. Feet First
        7. Sporting   14. Dirty Players   19. Naughty Monkeys
1. Kid's United 8. Sports Kids 15. Walking Legs   20. The Goal Monsters
2. Star Athletic 9. Quick Kickers 16. The Hungry Sharks
3. Heart Club   10. Dream Team   17. The Goal Monsters
4. All Sports   11. Great Movers 18. Naughty Monkeys
5. Fit City   12. Cambridge Flyers 19. The Terrible Tigers
6. Box Runners 13. The Non Starters 20. Feet First

 Compare this week to last week. Write.

This week Heart Club are third, but
last week they were first.

Vocabulary: ordinal numbers: *first* to *twentieth* **39**

Lock's sounds and spelling

1 39 ▶ **Watch the video. Watch again and practise.**

2 **Find and draw □, T or △. Say.**

Yesterday, it rained all day. They were bored inside. They decided to put on their boots and go outside! They skipped and jumped, danced and skated.

3 **Make sentences and say.**

> On Monday, I watched a film.

> On Tuesday, I danced with my friend.

> On Wednesday, …

dance *watch* climb **play**

skip *jump* chat **decide** clean

skate want

shout help

start

Show what you know

skipped	called	played
shouted	jumped	helped
decided	rained	skated

Lock & Key!

1 **Who is your favourite person in the story? Why?**

▶ What can a survey tell us?

1 🎧 41 **Listen and read. What's the survey about?**

What sports and activities are popular?

Which sports and activities do you do in your free time? A recent survey in the UK asked students between the ages of 8 and 12 years old the same question! Here are the results:

- 45% of children play football — that's almost half the children in the survey!
- Nearly a third of the children do swimming or diving — 30% in total.
- A quarter of the children go to a gym to do gymnastics or exercise.
- 18% of the children go running.
- Only 12% of the children play tennis.

2 **Read again and write the percentages. Read and answer.**

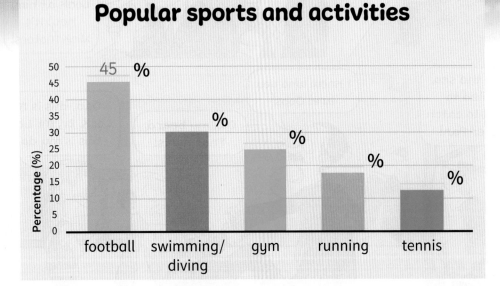

Popular sports and activities

45 %

(chart: football, swimming/diving, gym, running, tennis; y-axis: Percentage (%) 0–50)

1 Which sport is the most popular?

2 Which sport is the least popular?

3 Which activity do a quarter of the children do?

3 Which activities from the survey do you do? Tell a friend.

DID YOU KNOW...?
Table tennis player Hend Zaza, from Syria, was the youngest athlete at the Tokyo Olympics. She was just 12 years old!

4 **Read the survey results. What is the most popular after school activity?**

What are my classmates' favourite after school activities?

I asked 20 students in my class about their favourite after school activities. Here are the results of my survey:

- Half the class are members of the **sports club**. Of those 10 students, 50% play football, more than a quarter play tennis, and the rest go running.

- Six students in the class said their favourite after school activity is the **games club** – that's almost a third of the class. The most popular game in the club is chess.

- The other 20% of the class are members of the **drama club**.

By Priya

5 **Circle the words for these percentages in Activity 4. Write.**

50% = _____   33% = _____   25% = _____

Ready to write:

Go to Activity Book page 42.

Learning to write:
Percentages in words
A **quarter** of the children go to a gym.

6 **Calculate and complete the results of the survey.**

Let's do Maths!

Total number of students: ☐

1 football (5 students)   100 ÷ 20 = 5 x ⟨5⟩ = ⟨25⟩ %

2 tennis (3 students)   100 ÷ 20 = 5 x ☐ = ☐ %

3 running (2 students)   100 ÷ 20 = 5 x ☐ = ☐ %

4 games (6 students)   100 ÷ 20 = 5 x ☐ = ☐ %

5 drama (4 students)   100 ÷ 20 = 5 x ☐ = ☐ %

TOTAL = ☐ %

Project

Do your own survey and make a poster.

1 Play the game.

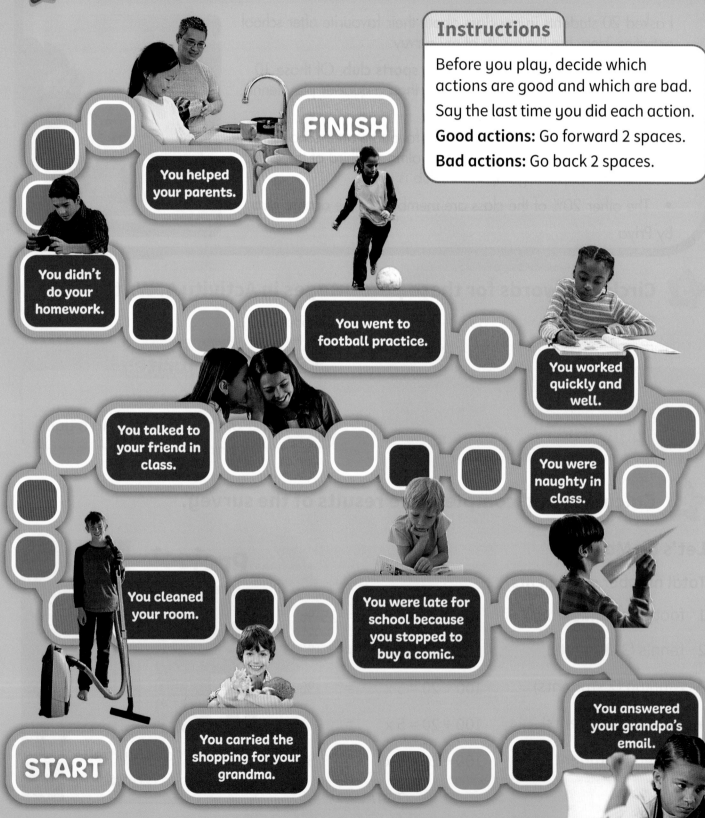

Instructions

Before you play, decide which actions are good and which are bad.

Say the last time you did each action.

Good actions: Go forward 2 spaces.

Bad actions: Go back 2 spaces.

FINISH

You helped your parents.

You didn't do your homework.

You went to football practice.

You worked quickly and well.

You talked to your friend in class.

You were naughty in class.

You cleaned your room.

You were late for school because you stopped to buy a comic.

You answered your grandpa's email.

START

You carried the shopping for your grandma.

2 🎧 42 **How did Mary go to these places? Listen and write a letter in each box. There is one example.**

 train [H]

 walking ☐

 bike ☐

 car ☐

 bus ☐

 boat ☐

 A

 B

 C

 D

 E

 F

 G

 H

Quiz

1. Where did Simon go on Thursday? (p28)
2. Who had lunch in bed in hospital? (p29)
3. Who took Lock's motorbike? (p33)
4. Which job is one of the most popular in the United States? (p34)
5. Who carried the chairs for the After school club? (p36)
6. Why did David point and shout? (p37)
7. What did Lock and Key drink at the school show? (p41)
8. What percentage is a half? (p43)

Simon Star

Expedition to Antarctica.

A famous explorer, Sir Ernest Shackleton, wanted to cross Antarctica. In 1914, he started the expedition, but ice closed around the ship. They took smaller boats and made a camp on the snow. They lost their ship when it went down under the ice and water.

They couldn't move because the weather was terrible. They caught fish and drank water which they got from snow. Later, they had to eat their dogs.

Shackleton and some of his men climbed over mountains of ice, found help and went back for the other men. Everybody came home two years after the start of their expedition. They didn't cross Antarctica.

 1 Look, think and answer. Read and check.

1 Who did Simon show his homework to?
2 Who did Simon write about?
3 Who was Shackleton?
4 How did Shackleton go to Antarctica?

 2 Find the past tense of these verbs in the text.

find   catch   take   go   make   get   can't   lost   have to   come

 3 Was it a good expedition? Why? Why not?

1 Read and match.

   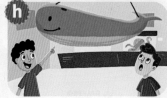

1 Last week, David's class went to a museum.

2 First, they walked round an exhibition about explorers.

3 They could read explorers' diaries so it was really exciting.

4 Before lunch, they made a poster about famous explorers.

5 After lunch, they found the museum shop and David got a toy polar bear for his sister.

6 In the afternoon, they went to an exhibition about sea animals.

7 Before they came home, David took a photograph of his friends.

8 At three o'clock, they caught the bus home.

f

2  Listen and answer.

1 When did David's class go to a museum?

They went to a museum last week.

3 Make sentences.

They were hungry so they ate sandwiches.

1 They were hungry		they couldn't find the museum.
2 They didn't take water with them		he got a toy from the shop.
3 The exhibition was really good	so	they ate sandwiches.
4 It was his sister's birthday		they came home late.
5 The children had to wait for the bus		they had a great time.
6 They lost their map		they were thirsty.

 **Look, think and answer. Listen and check.**

1 Which explorers are Simon and Alex talking about?
2 What was Cousteau's ship called?
3 Who did Alex write about?
4 What did Cousteau explore?

2 **Read and complete.**

Alex thinks that Shackleton's adventures were ¹ more difficult ²
Cousteau's, but Cousteau is ³ _____ famous for his work. Cousteau said we
have to be ⁴ _____ careful with the sea. Stella thinks Simon's homework was
⁵ _____ interesting ⁶ _____ hers. Lenny was happy because he did his
homework ⁷ _____ quickly than Simon and Alex.

3 **Find information and write about one of the explorers.**

Karen Darke   Matt Rutherford   Ed Stafford   Jessica Watson

Jessica Watson

STUDY

Cousteau is **more famous** for his work.
Our homework was **easier than** theirs.
Shackleton sailed **more slowly than** Cousteau.

48 **Language:** comparative adjectives and adverbs

1 What do you think? Tell a friend.

boring   exciting   dangerous
beautiful   difficult   easy

I think climbing is more dangerous than swimming.

 climbing    swimming

 Maths   Art

 horses    fish

 pop music   classical music

 badminton    table tennis

 photos   paintings

2 Now write four sentences.

I think badminton is more boring than table tennis.

3 🎵🎧 45 ▶ Complete. Listen and check.

trees   green   ~~mine~~   ours   his   strong

The world isn't ¹ mine ,
The world isn't yours.
The world isn't ² ,
The world isn't hers.
It's ours,
It's ³ !

Our world is tired, we're making mistakes,
We need our seas, we need our lakes.
Our world is weak, we can make it ⁴ ,
It needs our help. Listen to our song.

We must look after its forests and ⁵ ,
We must look after its rivers and seas.
We can make it better, we can make it ⁶ ,
This is our world, let's keep it clean.

4 🎵🎧 46 ▶ Sing the song. Do karaoke.

Lock's sounds and spelling

 1 🎧 47 ▶ **Watch the video. Watch again and practise.**

 2 **Find and underline the sound. Say.**

Circus girl in a purple skirt. Turn and surf around the world.

3 **Play the game.**

Circus girl went to the desert. She was very thirsty and dirty!

thirsty   dangerous   boring   slow   exciting
easy   difficult   interesting   quick   dirty

START→

Arctic

MISS A TURN

desert

mountains

forest

sea

GO BACK ONE SPACE

lake

circus

GO BACK TWO SPACES

world

FINISH

Show what you know

My favourite colour in the w ___ ld is p ___ ple.

Lock & Key!

1 Look, Key! I've got information about Nick Motors. He's on an adventure holiday in the countryside.

EXPLORE ADVENTURE

Good! These holidays are more exciting than holidays at the beach.

2 Look here. It says you can explore forests, rivers and beaches. Can we go, Lock? Please!

EXPLORE ADVENTURE

OK, Key. But we have to catch Nick Motors!

3 He came here yesterday. He caught a bus in the afternoon and had dinner at the Lakeside Restaurant.

LAKESIDE RESTAURANT

We can catch him easily, Lock. No problem.

EXPLORE ADVENTURE HOLIDAY CAMP

4 Excuse me. Do you know this man?

Oh yes! I gave him his breakfast this morning.

CAUTION WET FLOOR

Hmmm, but he's not here now.

Menu

5 Hello! What are you doing here, mr Key?

Hello, miss Rich. We're at work. We're trying to catch a thief.

I've got a message on my phone!

6 I don't understand. It says, 'Look behind you!'

He's got our bike! I need a holiday.

1 **What did Nick do at the holiday camp? Say three things.**

How can I stay safe outdoors?

1 🎧 49 **Listen and read. What are 'dos and don'ts'?**

check the weather!

Extreme heat and extreme cold can both be dangerous. Here are some 'dos and don'ts' for protecting yourself in hot and cold climates.

UV rays from the sun are dangerous and can cause sunburn. Use sun cream to protect your skin.

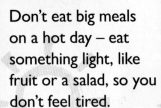

Without water, our bodies dehydrate. Drink lots of water to stay healthy in hot weather.

Don't eat big meals on a hot day – eat something light, like fruit or a salad, so you don't feel tired.

Wear warm clothes in cold weather, like a thick jumper, a coat, a scarf and a hat. Use thick socks and waterproof shoes to keep your feet warm and dry.

Don't go outside with wet hair. It feels cold and uncomfortable.

Eat plenty of vegetables when the weather is cold. This will help to keep your body strong and healthy.

2 **Read and complete the table.**

Dos and don'ts for hot weather	Dos and don'ts for cold weather
use sun cream	

3 **What activities do you do in hot and cold weather?**

DIDYOUKNOW...?
Over 50% of your body is water! You need to drink a lot of it to stay healthy.

5

4 **Read the leaflet. Make a list of things to take on a hiking trip.**

SAFETY TIPS: HIKING IN HOT WEATHER

Hiking is great fun, especially in the summer. Here are some tips to stay safe:

1 Drink lots of water to keep your body hydrated.
2 Wear sun cream to protect your skin from dangerous UV rays.
3 Wear light clothing so that you are comfortable.
4 Use insect repellent to protect yourself from insect bites.
5 Carry medicine in case you feel ill.

6 Don't go alone. Stay with your friends so you can look after each other.
7 Don't forget to take a mobile phone and a map. You don't want to get lost.

Stay safe and enjoy your hike!

5 **Underline the imperatives in Activity 4.**

Ready to write:

Go to Activity Book page 52.

Learning to write:

Imperatives
Wear warm clothes.
Don't eat big meals.

6 **Read the reasons and write the instructions.**

Dos and don'ts	Why?
Wear sun cream	1 To protect your skin from the sun.
	2 To be comfortable.
	3 To stay hydrated.
	4 In case you feel ill.
	5 So you don't get lost.
	6 To protect from insect bites.
	7 So you can look after each other.

Project

Make a safety poster.

6 Technology

the internet

email

screen

INTERNET NEWS

app

keyboard

mouse

DVD

button

laptop

1 🎧 50 Look, think and answer. Listen and check.

1 What's Stella talking about?

3 Who knows about computers?

2 Who wants to learn about computers?

4 Who's thinking about shopping?

2 🎧 51 Listen and repeat. Say the letter.

1 screen   screen – c

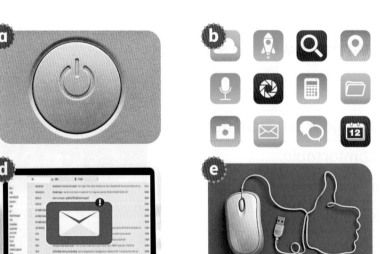

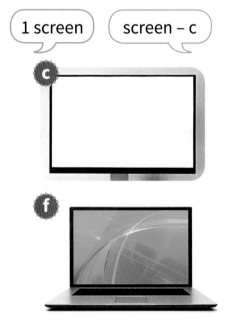

3 What technology do you use at home?

54   Vocabulary: technology

6

1 🎵🎧 52 ▶ Listen and match. 1 – e

Grandpa needs a new mobile, (No, I don't!)
With a music app. (A what?)
It's got songs and [1] **video clips**,
And he can learn to rap. (I can learn to WHAT?)

Grandpa needs a new mobile, (No, I don't!)
So he can [2] **text** his friends. (I can talk to my friends!)
He can take lots of [3] **photos**,
And play [4] **games** at weekends. (I go fishing at weekends!)

Grandpa! (I've got a DVD player at home!)
Grandpa! (I've got a nice camera!)
Grandpa! (And my old mobile phone works perfectly well!)
Grandpa needs a new mobile. (A new mobile phone!)

Grandpa needs a new mobile, (No, I don't!)
So he can [5] **plan** his day. (I've got a pen and paper!)
He can listen to lots of [6] **songs**,
And [7] **phone** or even play. (I haven't got time to play! I've got a radio!
I've got a nice camera! My old mobile phone works perfectly well! Hmph!)

2 🎵🎧 53 ▶ Sing the song. Do karaoke.

3 Ask and answer.

> Has your grandpa got a mobile phone?

> No, he hasn't.

> Can you use a computer?

> Yes, I can.

computer   TV   camera   the internet
mobile phone   email   e-book   laptop   app

 **1** 🎧 54 ▶ **Look, think and answer. Listen and check.**

1 Where did Grandma and Grandpa go yesterday?
2 What did they get?

3 What's their laptop called?
4 What problem have they got?

Today

Yesterday

LATEST MODELS
BEST PRICES
KBX4

 2 **Read and circle.**

Grandma and Grandpa went shopping yesterday. They ¹(**bought**)/ **thought** a laptop. They chose a KBX4 because Grandma ² **put** / **read** about it and the man in the shop ³ **chose** / **thought** it was better than the others. The man ⁴ **brought** / **knew** it home later. He took it out of the box, ⁵ **put** / **bought** it on the table and ⁶ **read** / **said** goodbye. He thought they ⁷ **chose** / **brought** the KBX4 because they ⁸ **knew** / **said** about computers!

 3 **Talk about the last time you went to the shops.**

Last time I went to the shops, I bought a book.

STUDY

choose ➜ chose	put ➜ put
buy ➜ bought	read ➜ read
bring ➜ brought	say ➜ said
know ➜ knew	think ➜ thought

Language: past simple irregular verbs

1 🎧 55 **Listen and correct the actions.**

Jim's got a new computer game called *Kid City*. The people in his game do different things every day. Look at what they did yesterday.

> 1 At seven o'clock, John got dressed.

> No. At seven o'clock, John got up.

Yesterday

2 **Ask and answer.**

> What time did Mary get dressed?

> She got dressed at eight o'clock.

3 **Write sentences about your day yesterday. Tell a friend.**

I got up at seven o'clock yesterday.

Lock's sounds and spelling

1  🎧 56 ▶ **Watch the video. Watch again and practise.**

2 **Find and draw ◯◯ , ◯ or △. Say.**

◯◯   △   ◯
Yesterday at four, they walked to the sea shore.

They brought a ball and did some sports.
And then they walked some more!

3 **Choose, ask and answer.**

What did you do yesterday at ten?   I talked to my grandma.

walk to (a place)   talk to (someone)   buy (something)   catch (the bus)
call (someone)   do sports   play with a ball

Yesterday at …

Show what you know

1 Look at the pictures. Describe what's happening.

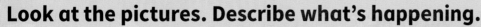

In picture 1, Lock and Key are having a video call.

How does technology help us?

1 🎧 58 **Listen and read. How can technology help the environment?**

Yesterday and today

In the past, people only used telephones to make phone calls. Today, we've got smartphones. They're more like small computers. We can use them to make calls, play games, send text messages and videos, take photos, and send emails.

People printed everything in the past – books, magazines and newspapers – and everyone read on paper. Now, a lot of people read news stories on the internet and buy e-books – electronic books that you read on a screen. It helps the environment because we use less paper.

People listened to music on 'personal stereos' in the past. They were cassette players with headphones that people carried with them in the street. Now, people listen to music on their smartphones.

---

2 **Read again and complete the diagram.**

```
        Past              Present
                  Both
  Read on paper   Use phones to   Use phones to play games,
                  make calls      take photos and send messages
```

3 **Do you prefer old or new technology? Why?**

4 Read the biography. Name three amazing inventions.

George Devol was born in 1912. He was an American inventor.

In 1954, he invented the first robot. He called it 'Unimate'. It was a robotic arm that moved things.

He heard the word 'robot' in a play when he was nine years old. That was 33 years before he made his robot arm.

In the 1940s, he invented other things, too, including an automatic door that opened when people walked near it, and a machine that cooked hot dogs.

George Devol died in 2011. He was 99 years old.

5 Underline the regular past tense verbs in Activity 4. Circle the irregular past tense verbs.

Ready to write:

Go to Activity Book page 60.

Learning to write:

Past tense verbs

People **printed** everything in the past.

Everybody **read** on paper.

6 Complete the timeline. Talk about your favourite invention.

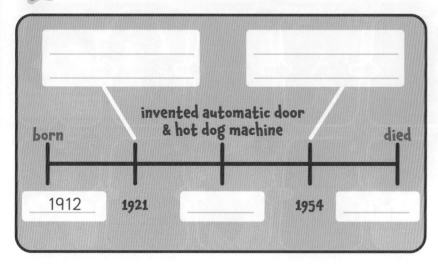

invented automatic door & hot dog machine

born _____ _____ died

1912   1921   _____   1954   _____

Project

Interview your family about technology in the past.

Review Units 5 and 6

1 Play the game. What did they do yesterday?

Instructions

1 Roll the dice and move around the board.
2 Say what each person did yesterday.
3 If your sentence is correct, stay where you are.
4 If your sentence is wrong, go back to where you were.

2 **Read the story and complete the sentences. Use 1, 2 or 3 words.**

Shopping trip

Last Wednesday, Alex went shopping with his mother, Pat. They went to town by bus and had a burger in a café before they went to the shops. Alex's mum wanted to buy a new bike for his younger sister, Jill. It was her birthday on Friday. The name of the toy shop was 'Pete's Toys'. They bought Jill a new red bike and took it home on the bus.

1 Alex and ⬡ his ⬡ mother went shopping last Wednesday.

2 They ate ⬡ ⬡ in a café.

3 Jill is Alex's ⬡.

4 They bought Jill ⬡ ⬡ ⬡.

5 On Friday, it was ⬡ birthday.

6 Jill's bike was ⬡.

7 They went home ⬡ ⬡ ⬡.

Quiz

1 How did Shackleton and his men lose their ship? (p46)

2 What did David get for his sister? (p47)

3 Where did Nick Motors have dinner? (p51)

4 Name three things to do to stay safe in hot weather. (p52)

5 Which computer did Grandma and Grandpa buy? (p56)

6 What time did Mary catch the bus yesterday? (p57)

7 What did Nick Motors write? (p59)

8 Name an invention that helps the environment. (p60)

7 At the zoo

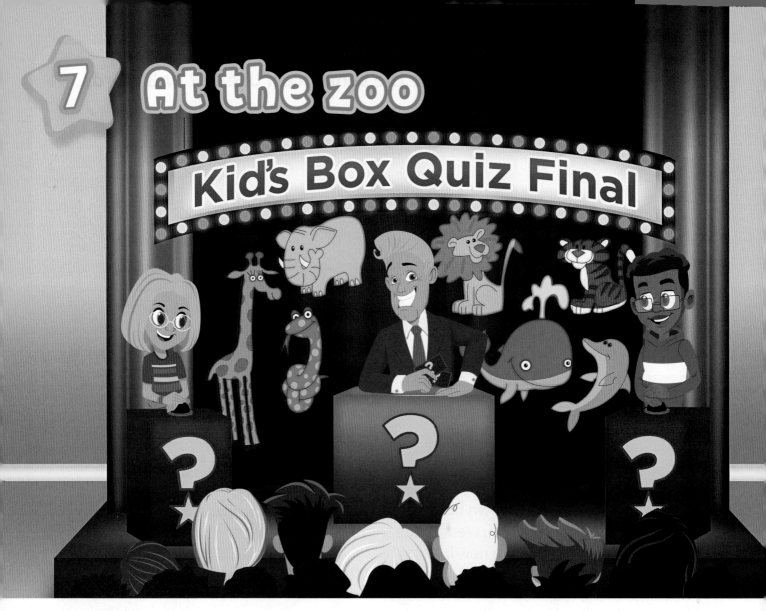

Kid's Box Quiz Final

 🎧 59 **Look, think and answer. Listen and check.**

1 What are Lenny and Stella doing?
2 Who's asking the questions?

3 What's the quiz about?
4 Who do you think is winning?

2 🎧 60 **Listen and say 'yes' or 'no'.**

1 Lenny thinks the most exciting animal is the giraffe.

No.

 **Talk about your family.**

My dad's the quickest at walking.

My sister's the best at Maths.

STUDY

quick ➜ the **quickest**
big ➜ the **biggest**
exciting ➜ the **most exciting**
beautiful ➜ the **most beautiful**
good ➜ the **best**

Language: superlative adjectives

1 Read and correct the sentences.

7

Fred's blog

Animals are one of the most interesting things to watch and study. A lot of people think that elephants are the biggest animals in the world, but the biggest animals are blue whales. They're the longest, biggest and the loudest of all animals. They're louder than planes.

One of the smallest animals in the world is a lizard.

It's between one and two centimetres long. The quickest animal is a bird which can fly at more than 300 kilometres an hour.

The cleverest animals are humans – that's us! Some people think that monkeys are the second cleverest, but they aren't. Dolphins are cleverer than monkeys.

My favourite animals are tigers. I think they're the most exciting and the most beautiful animals.

1 Kangaroos are the biggest animals.

> Blue whales are the biggest animals.

2 Bears are the loudest animals.
3 One of the smallest animals in the world is a rabbit.
4 The quickest animal is a lizard.
5 Monkeys are the second cleverest animals.
6 Fred thinks pandas are the most exciting animals.

2 What do you think? Talk to a friend and write.

> I think the shark is the most dangerous.

| beautiful exciting boring |
| clever ugly dangerous |

> I think the shark is the cleverest.

I think the rabbit is the most boring animal.

Language: superlative adjectives   65

1 🎧 61 ▶ Look, think and answer. Listen and check.

1 Where did the children go?

2 Who did Suzy give her picture to?

3 What animals did they feed?

4 Which animal did Simon like the best?

| drew | came | drove | saw | swam | slept | went |
| flew | bought | sat | caught | ate | ran | fed |

LOOK

 out of   into   around/round   along

2 🎧 62 Listen and say the letter.

1 Mr Star drove the children to the zoo.   a

3 Can you remember? Ask and answer.

What did the lizard catch?   It caught a fly.

STUDY

What **did** he **buy**?

He **bought** a toy parrot.

He **didn't buy** an ice cream.

Language: past simple irregular verbs

1 **Listen and do the actions.**

2 64–65 ▶ **Listen and sing. Do karaoke.**

The elephants drank, drank, drank,
The parrots flew, flew, flew,
The dolphins swam, swam, swam,
At the zoo, zoo, zoo.

The elephants drank, drank, drank,
The parrots flew, flew, flew,
The dolphins swam, swam, swam,
At the zoo, zoo, zoo.

What did you do,
What did you do,
What did you do,
When you saw, saw, saw them
At the zoo, zoo, zoo?

The monkeys ate, ate, ate,
The children drew, drew, drew,
The lions slept, slept, slept,
At the zoo, zoo, zoo.

The monkeys ate, ate, ate,
The children drew, drew, drew,
The lions slept, slept, slept,
At the zoo, zoo, zoo.

What did you do,
What did you do,
What did you do,
When you saw, saw, saw them
At the zoo, zoo, zoo?

When you saw, saw, saw them
At the zoo, zoo, zoo?

3 **Write another verse for the song.**

The crocodiles smiled , smiled , smiled ,
The giraffes _____ , _____ , _____ ,
The tigers _____ , _____ , _____ ,
At the zoo, zoo, zoo.

~~smile~~   dance
jump   laugh
climb   hop

Language: past simple irregular and regular verbs   **67**

1 🎧 66 ▶ **Watch the video. Watch again and practise.**

2 **Find and underline the sounds. Say.**

Yesterday, they fl<u>ew</u> to the new rescue zoo to see the baboon.

He swam in the pool and stood on one foot.

He stole a balloon and hid in the wood.

3 **Look and find the differences. Say.**

a

b

In picture a, there's a brown bear in the tree.

In picture b, there's a blue bear in the tree.

Show what you know

good	stood
baboon	zoo
flew	foot
blue	wood

1 Why do you think Nick Motors is the most wanted man in town?

How are life cycles different?

1 **Look at the timeline. Which animals have the shortest and the longest lifespans?**

 mouse: 1 year

 elephant: 70 years

 mayfly: 1 day

 tiger: 25 years

Greenland shark: 200–400 years

2 🎧 68 **Listen and read. Label the diagram.**

ANIMAL LIFE CYCLES

Different animals have different lifespans. A mayfly lives for just one day, but some sharks can live for over 200 years!

Giant tortoises live on the Galápagos Islands in the Pacific Ocean. They can live for a very long time. The oldest giant tortoises are over 180 years old!

First, the mother tortoise lays an **egg**. When a baby tortoise is born, it's called a **hatchling**. They grow for a few years and become a **juvenile** or child. Then they grow for another 25 to 40 years and become an **adult**.

1 egg

 2

 4

 3

3 **What are the stages in a human life cycle? How long is each stage? Think and say.**

DIDYOUKNOW...?
Giant tortoises can sleep for 16 hours a day!

Science: How are life cycles different? | 🛡 critical thinking

4 **Read the report on Greenland sharks. Underline three amazing facts.**

The amazing Greenland shark

The Greenland shark is a fish. It lives in the Arctic Ocean, which is very cold. It has one of the longest lifespans — it can live for 400 years!

The Greenland shark is huge. Some are over six metres long and weigh 1,000 kilograms! It's the largest fish in the Arctic Ocean and it swims very slowly.

The Greenland shark eats meat, but it doesn't need to hunt. That's because it can eat dead fish and seals!

If you catch a Greenland shark, do not eat it. Its meat is poisonous!

5 **Circle the exclamation marks in Activity 4.**

Ready to write:

Go to Activity Book page 70.

Learning to write:

Exclamation marks
A mayfly lives for just one day!

6 **How long is the human lifespan? What can you do to live longer? Talk to a friend and write.**

The human lifespan is about _____ years.
Ideas to keep healthy and live a long life:
1   Eat lots of fruit and vegetables.
2
3
4

Project

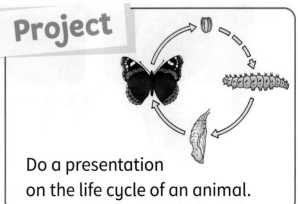

Do a presentation on the life cycle of an animal.

8 Let's party!

box
cup
soup
cheese
bottle
sandwich
vegetables
salad
bowl
pasta
glass

1 🎧 69 **Look, think and answer. Listen and check.**

1 Whose birthday is it today?
2 What are the grown-ups doing?

3 What kind of sandwiches are there?
4 Who's thirsty?

2 🎧 70 **Listen and say the letter.**

1 A bowl of salad.   b

a
b
c
d
e
f
g
h

3 **What do you like to eat at parties?**

Language: expressions of quantity

1  71 Listen and say the letter.

1 Can you take these dirty cups to the kitchen, please, children? b

a He wants her to make a cheese sandwich.

b She wants them to take the cups to the kitchen.

c He wants him to pass the bowl of salad.

d She wants him to hold the glass.

e They want her to open the bottle of lemonade.

f He wants them to put the glasses on the table.

2 Read and correct the sentences.

Paul's a teenager and today he's at home with his younger brother and sister. He wants to make lunch for his mum and dad. He wants his brother and sister to help him. He wants Vicky to make a bowl of noodles and then he wants her to make some tomato sauce. He wants Jack to take a plate of sandwiches and a bottle of lemonade to the table. After lunch, he wants him to make a cup of coffee for their parents. Paul wants to sit down and watch TV with a glass of juice. His brother and sister aren't happy, they're angry. They want Paul to help them.

1 Paul wants his mum and dad to help him.
2 He wants Vicky to make a bowl of salad.
3 He wants her to make some tomato soup.
4 Paul wants Jack to take a plate of pancakes to the table.
5 He wants him to make a cup of coffee for their aunt and uncle.

Language: *want someone to (do something)*   73

Look, think and answer. Listen and check.

1 What are the children doing?
2 Who's first?

3 Who's last?
4 Who's walking?

 **Listen and say the name.**

1 He's jumping the most quickly.

Alex.

 Describe the picture.

Suzy's jumping the most slowly.

STUDY

quickly → the **most quickly**
slowly → the **most slowly**
well → the **best**
badly → the **worst**

Language: superlative adverbs

1 Look and find the differences. Say.

In picture b, the clown's drinking a milkshake.

2 ♫🎧 74 ▶ Complete the song. Listen and check.

made   ate   wore   ~~said~~   drank   danced   gave   was

We had soup, we had pasta,
We had salads and cheese.
We all wanted more,
We all ¹ said 'please'.
We ²   presents,
And cards which we ³   .
We ⁴   fancy dress,
We ⁵   and we played ...

The party was good,
The party ⁶   great.
And now it's time to fly.
The party was good,
The party was great.
We'll see you soon, goodbye.

The drinks we ⁷   ,
The food we ⁸   .
The party was good,
The party was great.
We gave presents ...

Now the party's over,
Now it's time to fly.
See you soon, goodbye.

3 ♫🎧 75 ▶ Sing the song. Do karaoke.

1 🎧 76 ▶ **Watch the video. Watch again and practise.**

 2 **Find and count the sounds. Say.**

The girl with curly hair skated while a very big bear waited.

A sloth with a spoon swam in the pool with a baboon.

They did sports, rode bikes, and had good fun all night.

They danced, played and walked, ate noodles and talked.

3 **Describe and guess.**

She rode a bike quickly.

Circus girl!

Yesterday

CIRCUS

1 **Look back at the Lock and Key stories. Which is your favourite? Why?**

Story: unit language in context   77

How can we write poetry?

1 🎧 78 **Listen and read. Which poem talks about food?**

Poetry competition

Thank you to everyone who sent us their poems for the school poetry competition. We asked you to write a rhyming poem or an acrostic poem about celebrations. Here are this year's competition winners!

a Street party

Watch the people as they sing,
And dance under the dragon's wing.
A street party to mark the day,
A brand new year the Chinese way.

b CAKE

Congratulations for today!
Are you feeling happy?
Kind words and hugs from all your friends.
Eat some cake and celebrate!

2 **Read and match the poems with their descriptions.**

1 ☐

An **acrostic** is a poem where the first letter of each line spells a word. It's called a 'topic word' because the topic of the poem is always connected to the word. Acrostic poems don't need to rhyme.

2 ☐

A **rhyming** poem uses words with the same sound – like 'fun' and 'sun', or 'bread' and 'red' – at the end of each line. Sometimes the first two lines rhyme, and then the next two lines rhyme with a different sound. Sometimes the first and third lines, or the second and fourth lines rhyme.

3 **Which is your favourite poem? Why?**

DID YOU KNOW...?

Poems can be long or short.
The Scottish poet George MacDonald wrote a poem with only two words: 'Come home'.

4 **Read the poem. What is it about?**

Summer is my favourite time,
Under the bright sun.
Nice weather all day long.
New plans for holiday fun.
Young, free and happy!

5 **Circle the rhyming words in Activity 4.**

Ready to write:

Go to Activity Book page 78.

Learning to write:

Rhyming words
Watch the people as they **sing**,
And dance under the dragon's **wing**.

6 **Write the topic word from the poem. Complete the mind map with words related to the topic.**

beach

S _ _ _ _ _

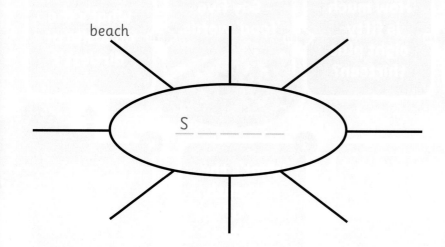

Project

Make a class anthology of poems.

Review Units 7 and 8

1 Play the game.

Instructions

1 Play in groups of three or four.

2 Move and answer the questions. You only have 30 seconds.

- Right answer: stay.
- Wrong answer: go back one space.

18 What's the opposite of 'outside'?

19 What's the past of 'drive'?

20 Say five 'technology' words.

FINISH

17 How much is forty-three plus eighteen?

16 Say five 'transport' words.

15 What's the past of 'know'?

14 What kind of animals can fly?

10 Say five 'job' words.

11 What's the past of 'choose'?

12 Say five 'school' words.

13 Which is the tallest animal?

9 What's the opposite of 'into'?

8 What's the past of 'think'?

7 How much is fifty-eight plus thirteen?

6 Say five 'food' words.

5 What's the opposite of 'dirtiest'?

START

1 Which animal lives in Antarctica?

2 Name five animals you can see at the zoo.

3 What's the fifteenth letter of the alphabet?

4 Say five 'clothes' words.

Tell the story.

> Peter got up and got ready. He was sad. He wanted to play football outside, but the weather was terrible …

 Now write the story.

Peter got up and got ready. He was sad. He wanted to play football outside, but the weather was terrible.

1. Which is the loudest of all animals? (p65)

2. Who drove the children to the zoo? (p66)

3. What did Nick Motors take from the zoo? (p69)

4. Which animal has a life cycle of one day? (p70)

5. What does Paul want Jack to take to the table? (p73)

6. Who jumped the most slowly in the sack race? (p74)

7. Which three things did Nick Motors want to give the tiger? (p77)

8. What type of poem has a topic word? (p78)

1 Look at the photos. What's happening? Why?

2 🎧 79 **Listen and say the letter.**

 3 **Read and complete.**

> our teacher.   them a letter.
> and smile at them.   ~~they help us.~~
> say thank you.   give them a picture.

We say thank you to people when …

they help us.

1 We say thank you to people when …
2 We can give someone a present to …
3 When people help us, we can say thank you …
4 When we enjoy a school lesson, we can say thank you to …
5 When we want to say thank you to people, we can …
6 To say thank you to someone, we can sometimes write …

 4 **When do you say thank you?**

Units 3&4 Values Be kind

1 🎧 80 **Read and think. Say 'yes' or 'no'. Listen and check.**

1 We can give our seat to older people on the bus.
2 It's bad to help younger children with a problem.
3 We can ask old people to carry our bags.
4 We can help our family to water the plants.

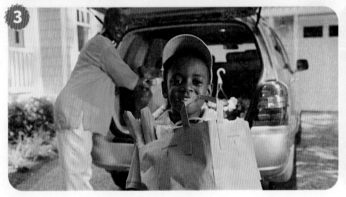

 Read and match.

1 If we see old people on a bus or train, we can …

2 If we see a small child with a problem, we can …

3 If we see an older person with a shopping bag, we can …

4 We can help our parents when we see something …

a carry it for them.

b is difficult for them.

c try to help them.

d stand up and give them our seat.

 How do you help other people?

1 🎧 81 Read and think. Say 'yes' or 'no'. Listen and check.

1 You can play near busy roads.
2 You can cross the road between cars.
3 You must stop, look and listen before you cross the road.
4 You must wear a helmet when you ride a bike.

2 Read and complete.

use it to cross the road.   can't see you.   busy roads.
~~ride a bike.~~   before you cross the road.

> Remember to put on a helmet when you …

1 Remember to put on a helmet when you …
2 Don't stand between cars when you cross the road. Drivers …
3 Don't play next to …
4 Remember to stop, look and listen …
5 When there is a zebra crossing, always …

> ride a bike.

3 How do you stay safe?

1 🎧 82 **Read and think. Say 'yes' or 'no'. Listen and check.**

1 We must put plastic and paper into special bins.
2 We mustn't recycle glass.
3 We can make things from old clothes.
4 We mustn't recycle clothes.

2 **Read and match.**

1 When we can't reuse things, we …
2 Make plastic bottles smaller …
3 Always put paper, glass, plastic and cans …
4 We can make new things …

a from old clothes.
b into the right recycling bins.
c before you recycle them.
d can sometimes recycle them.

3 **What do you recycle?**

Grammar reference

Grandpa Star's older than Mr Star.
The dog's bigger than the cat.
Uncle Fred's funnier than Aunt May.

She always has to work at the weekend.
He sometimes has to get up at five o'clock.
He never has to do his homework on Saturday.

He's / She's the teacher who's wearing a red sweater.
They're the girls who are skipping.

What do you / they want to learn to do? What do you / they want to learn how to do? What does he / she want to learn to do?	I / We / They want to learn to paint. I / We / They don't want to learn how to roller skate. He / She wants to learn to dance. He / She doesn't want to learn how to ride a horse.
What's the Activity Centre?	It's a place where you can learn to swim.

quick → quickly loud → loudly	They're running quickly. He's shouting loudly.

I / You / He / She / It / We / They	had / didn't have lunch at school.
Did you see the dentist last year? Did he / she eat chocolate cake?	Yes, I did. / No, I didn't. Yes, he / she did. / No, he / she didn't.
How many ice creams did you eat?	I ate two ice creams. / I didn't eat an ice cream.

Her mum gave her medicine I had a drink They ate a sandwich	because	she had a headache. I was hot. they were hungry.

What did Alex need? Where did she live? Who did Mr Burke stop? What did Simon carry?	Alex needed a hat and a scarf. She lived in a big town. Mr Burke stopped Simon. Simon carried the boxes.

| They were hungry
It was cold
I couldn't find my map | so | they ate an apple.
they had a hot drink.
I got lost. |

| interesting → more interesting
famous → more famous
difficult → more difficult | This film is more interesting than that one.
She is more famous than him.
Maths is more difficult than English. |
| slowly → more slowly
carefully → more carefully | My bike goes more slowly than yours.
He rides his bike more carefully than her. |

| What did you buy?
Where did he put the mouse?
What did they think?
What did she know? | I bought / didn't buy a new laptop.
He put / didn't put it on the table.
They thought / didn't think the internet was slow.
She knew / didn't know the song on the radio. |

| quick → quicker → the quickest
beautiful → more beautiful → the most beautiful
good → better → the best | It's the quickest lizard in the world.
Whales are the most beautiful animals.
I think rabbits are the best pets. |

| What did you eat?
What did he / she see?
Where did they / we swim? | I ate / didn't eat the cake.
He / She saw / didn't see a dolphin.
They / We swam / didn't swim in the sea. |

| a bottle of lemonade
a bowl of salad | a box of eggs
a cup of tea | a glass of juice |

| I / You / We / They
He / She | want
wants | me / you / her / him / us / them | to wash the dishes.
to open the door. |

| slowly → more slowly → the most slowly
carefully → more carefully → the most carefully | The woman's walking the most slowly.
The boys are riding the most carefully. |

Movers Listening

1 🎧 83 **Read and write your ideas. Listen, write and check.**

	Our ideas	Answers
Club is opposite:		the library
Get there by:		
Number of activities:		
Activity on Sunday:		
Club closed on:		
Club shop sells:		

2 🎧 84 **Listen and write. There is one example.**

New class: _climbing_

1 Name of sports club: _____

2 The bus stop is next to: _____

3 Number of walls: _____

4 Activity on Wednesday: _____

5 Must bring: _____

A new class

Movers Listening

1 🎧 85 **Listen and circle. Use the code.** | Answer = orange | | Distractor = purple |

1 What's Paul's favourite hobby?

2 Where does Lucy go riding?

3 What sport does Mr Brown teach after school?

4 Whose guitar is it?

5 Where are Charlie and his family going at the weekend?

2 🎧 86 🐵 **Jack is telling his aunt about the new activities his friends are doing. What activities are they doing?**

Listen and write a letter in each box. There is one example.

 Sally F   Vicky

 Jack   Suzy

 Fred   Jim

 A    B    C    D

 E    F    G    H

Movers Reading and Writing

1 Read. Find and colour the answers.

1 I love dolphins.
2 What's the weather like?
3 Fred's at the bus station.
4 Clare is in bed with a temperature.
5 Would you like a sandwich?

6 Whose roller skates are those?
7 Were there many children at the picnic?
8 Did you like the film?
9 There was a rainbow this morning.
10 Let's go to the pool!

(They're mine.) (How beautiful!) (So do I!) (Yes, please.) (It's wet.)

(No, he isn't.) (I can't today.) (It was OK.) (Yes, lots.) (Oh, dear!)

2 Read the text and choose the best answer.

Example

Peter: Hi, Lily. You weren't in class this morning.

Lily: A Yes, I am.
 B I was sick.
 C No, I don't.

Questions

1 **Peter:** What's the matter? Have you got a cold?
 Lily: A No, I don't want one.
  B Yes, I'm fine now, thank you.
  C No, I've got an earache.

2 **Peter:** Did you see a doctor?
 Lily: A I'm going now.
  B No, I'm not better.
  C It's at 11 o'clock.

3 **Peter:** Is your doctor called Mrs Glass? She's very nice.
 Lily: A Yes, that's OK.
  B Yes, that's right.
  C Yes, she's very well.

4 **Peter:** Shall I come and visit you at home after the doctor's?
 Lily: A Yes, please.
  B No, it isn't my address.
  C Yes, it's here.

5 **Peter:** I can show you what we did in class today.
 Lily: A I'd love some.
  B I didn't see it.
  C I'd like that, thanks.

6 **Peter:** Let's go to the cinema when you're better.
 Lily: A It's the best!
  B That's a good idea!
  C It was OK!

Movers Reading and Writing

1 Read and complete. Tick (✓) the best title.

pancakes   scarf   white   family   dog   ~~temperature~~   road

Jack's mum woke him up on Sunday morning. She wanted Jack to take the dog for a walk because she had a ___temperature___ and was sick. Jack looked out of his window. There was snow on the (1) _____ . He wanted to stay in bed! Jack got dressed and put on his (2) _____ . He walked very slowly to the park. He didn't like cold weather. The park was very different with snow. It was quiet and (3) _____ .

Behind some trees, a girl waved at him. It was his school friend, Vicky. She was with her (4) _____ . 'Hi, Jack,' she said. 'We're having a breakfast picnic in the snow!' Jack had some (5) _____ to eat and drank some hot tea. Now he wasn't cold. 'What are you doing in the park at this time?' asked Vicky. 'Oh, no!' laughed Jack, 'I didn't bring my (6) _____ !'

Cold weather ☐   Dogs love parks ☐   Breakfast in the park ☐

2 Read the story. Choose a word from the box. Write the correct word next to numbers 1–5. There is one example.

Julia's classmates were happy. It was the last day of ___school___ before the holidays. Their teacher, Miss White, invited all the families to watch the children play and sing in their (1) _____ . The children wore black trousers and jackets. They all had (2) _____ . 'Wow! You are all pop stars!' Miss White told them when she saw them.

Julia was sad. Her grandmother couldn't come to the school because she was in (3) _____ . 'I know,' said Julia's friend, Jordan. 'I can video the band and put it on the school (4) _____ . Then your grandma can watch it on a tablet.' 'That's a great idea, Jordan,' said Miss White.

Some children sang and some played the guitar. Julia and Jordan played the piano. After school, Julia went to the hospital with her parents. They showed the video to Julia's grandmother and her grandmother started to (5) _____ . 'I think you're better now,' said Julia and everyone laughed.

school	running	hospital
sing	doctor	band
sunglasses	kitchen	website

(6) Now choose the best name for the story. Tick (✓) one box.

Pop stars visit the hospital ☐

A video for Grandma ☐

Everyone can sing! ☐

Movers Reading and Writing

1 **Choose and circle 9 words. Play *Bingo!***

> fly   drive   countryside   enjoy   phone   visit
> present   surprise   travel   meet   beach   breakfast

2  **Look at the pictures and read the story. Write some words to complete the sentences about the story. You can use 1, 2 or 3 words.**

Grandpa's birthday surprise!

On Saturday, Ben's grandpa phoned. 'Come and visit,' he said. 'It's my birthday on Sunday!'

Mum and Ben drove to Grandpa's house on Sunday morning. Grandpa lived near a farm and Ben loved looking at all the animals in the fields. Ben and his mum sang 'Happy Birthday' when he opened the door and Mum made pancakes for breakfast. Grandpa was a little sad he didn't get a present, but he enjoyed the pancakes.

Examples

Grandpa phoned Ben to talk about his _____birthday_____.

On Sunday morning, Ben and his mum visited his _____grandpa_____.

Questions

1 Grandpa had _____ for breakfast.

2 Ben and his mum didn't give Grandpa a _____.

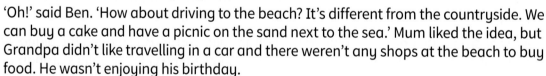

'What's the matter with Grandpa?' Ben asked his mum.

'I think he wants a birthday surprise!'

'Oh!' said Ben. 'How about driving to the beach? It's different from the countryside. We can buy a cake and have a picnic on the sand next to the sea.' Mum liked the idea, but Grandpa didn't like travelling in a car and there weren't any shops at the beach to buy food. He wasn't enjoying his birthday.

3 Ben and his mum decided to take Grandpa to the _____.

4 They went by _____, but Grandpa didn't enjoy it.

5 They couldn't have a picnic because the beach didn't have _____.

Then Mum had an idea. 'Let's go,' she said. 'I've got a friend I want you to meet!'

Mum's friend gave flying lessons at a small airport near the beach. A man in a green jacket and hat came to say hello. He had a helicopter and took them all for a ride in it.

'What a surprise!' said Grandpa. 'This is the best birthday present!' Ben and Mum enjoyed it, too.

6 Mum took Ben and Grandpa to an _____ to meet her friend.

7 Everyone loved flying in the _____.

Movers Reading and Writing

1 Look, read and correct.

hungry

Example: The clown is ~~thirsty~~.

1   The clown is drinking lemonade.

2   The pirate has got a moustache.

2 Look and read and write.

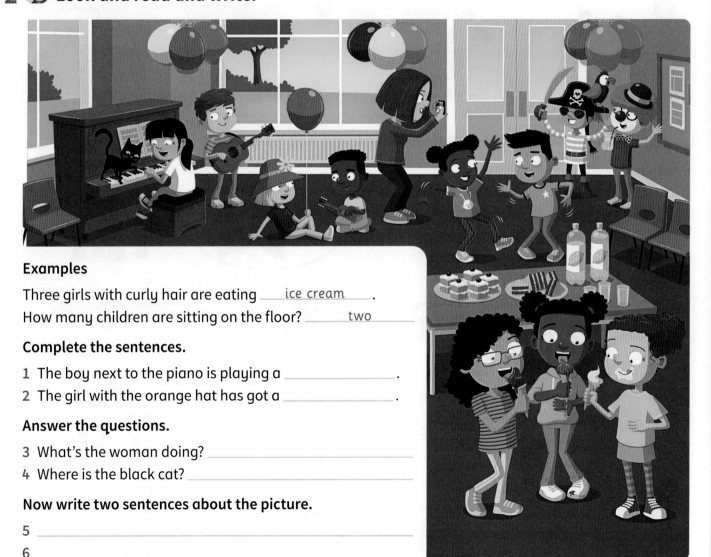

Examples

Three girls with curly hair are eating _____ice cream_____ .

How many children are sitting on the floor? _____ two _____

Complete the sentences.

1   The boy next to the piano is playing a _____ .

2   The girl with the orange hat has got a _____ .

Answer the questions.

3   What's the woman doing? _____

4   Where is the black cat? _____

Now write two sentences about the picture.

5   _____

6   _____

Movers Speaking

1 🎧 87 Listen and write '1' or '2'.

A — 2 , 1

B

C

D

E

F

2 🐵 Look. Circle the one that is different and say why.

Example

1

2

3

Movers Speaking

1 🎧 88 **Unscramble and write the questions. Listen and number.**

A school you do after ? Where go

B do What do ? sports you

C you weekend What do ? last did

D lives you Who ? with

E parties at What eat you ? do

F your What hobbies are ?

A Where do you go after school? ☐

B _____ ☐

C _____ ☐

D _____ ☐

E _____ 1

F _____ ☐

2 🐵 **Now interview a friend.**

Thanks and Acknowledgements

Authors' thanks

Many thanks to everyone at Cambridge University Press for their dedication and hard work, and in particular to:

Liane Grainger and Lynn Townsend for supervising the whole project and guiding us calmly through the storms.

Eve Conway for her astute observations and great editorial judgement. Thanks for all the hard work and great result.

We would also like to thank all our pupils and colleagues, past, present and future, at Star English academy in Murcia, especially Jim Kelly for his friendship and support throughout the years.

Dedications

For Teresa and Giuseppe Vincenti, for their wholehearted support and encouragement, with much love and thanks. – CN

To my great friends from the Levante: to Javi, Maria José and Laura, and to Jim Kelly. It's always a pleasure to spend time with good friends. – MT

The authors and publishers acknowledge the following sources of copyright material and are grateful for the permissions granted. While every effort has been made, it has not always been possible to identify the sources of all the material used, or to trace all copyright holders. If any omissions are brought to our notice, we will be happy to include the appropriate acknowledgements on reprinting and in the next update to the digital edition, as applicable.

Key: U = Unit

Photography

The following photos are sourced from Getty Images.

U0: Anna Erastova/iStock/Getty Images Plus; **U1:** Nickbeer/iStock/Getty Images Plus; clubfoto/iStock/Getty Images Plus; SW Productions/Photodisc; Halfpoint/iStock/Getty Images Plus; Geber86/E+; Westend61; Halfpoint/iStock/Getty Images Plus; Comstock/Stockbyte; Adene Sanchez/E+; Prostock-Studio/iStock/Getty Images Plus; Johner Images; PeopleImages/iStock/Getty Images Plus; Maskot; Cavan Images; Thomas Barwick/DigitalVision; Aleksandr Zubkov/Moment; enjoynz/DigitalVision Vectors; LuckyTD/iStock/Getty Images Plus; Cyndi Monaghan/Moment; **U2:** vernonwiley/E+; Sally Anscombe/Moment; SerrNovik/iStock/Getty Images Plus; Stuart Ashley/DigitalVision; monkeybusinessimages/iStock/Getty Images Plus; Daisy-Daisy/iStock/Getty Images Plus; Marc Romanelli; noblige/iStock/Getty Images Plus; Sino Images/500px Asia; Alistair Berg/DigitalVision; FatCamera/iStock/Getty Images Plus; robertprzybysz/iStock/Getty Images Plus; Westend61; ISMODE/iStock/Getty Images Plus; Yukobo/iStock/Getty Images Plus; Kolopach/iStock/Getty Images Plus; Bigmouse108/iStock/Getty Images Plus; KanKhem/iStock/Getty Images Plus; Anna Erastova/iStock/Getty Images Plus; Westend61; **U3:** baona/iStock/Getty Images Plus; alphaspirit/iStock/Getty Images Plus; wilpunt/E+; Westend61; DiMaggio/Kalish/The Image Bank; Werner Dieterich; Valerie Loiseleux/iStock/Getty Images Plus; pijama61/DigitalVision Vectors; Anna Erastova/iStock/Getty Images Plus; santima.studio/iStock/Getty Images Plus; **U4:** Westend61; Alex Potemkin/E+; Ilona Nagy/Moment; Daly and Newton/The Image Bank; BunnyHollywood/E+; Sollina Images; Stephen Simpson/Stone; andresr/E+; BraunS/E+; FatCamera/E+; vgajic/E+; Motortion/iStock/Getty Images Plus; DGLimages/iStock/Getty Images Plus; Anna Erastova/iStock/Getty Images Plus; Lawkeeper/iStock/Getty Images Plus; **U5:** Mike Hill/stone; Digital Vision; Moussa81/iStock/Getty Images Plus; ozgurcankaya/E+; DaniloAndjus/E+; AlesVeluscek/E+; Westend61; dejan Jekic/iStock/Getty Images Plus; Cavan Images; Richard Hutchings/Corbis Documentary; Anna Erastova/iStock/Getty Images Plus; Anastasia Vintovkina/iStock/Getty Images Plus; MicrovOne/iStock/Getty Images Plus; **U6:** Yuichiro Chino/Moment; solarisimages/iStock/Getty Images Plus; bamlou/DigitalVision Vectors; Kwanchai Lerttanapunyaporn/EyeEm; juststock/iStock/Getty Images Plus; mbortolino/E+; skegbydave/E+; Jose Luis Pelaez Inc/DigitalVision; TonyBaggett/iStock/Getty Images Plus; jayk7/Moment; 3alexd/iStock/Getty Images Plus; MoMo Productions/DigitalVision; Kraig Scarbinsky/DigitalVision; imtmphoto/iStock/Getty Images Plus; Kkolosov/iStock/Getty Images Plus; Larissa Veronesi/Moment; Image Source; skynesher/E+; George Doyle/Stockbyte; Fuse/Corbis; Ihor Bulyhin/iStock/Getty Images Plus; Julie Toy/Stone; Seamind Panadda/EyeEm; Rubberball/Mike Kemp/Brand X Pictures; Studio Paggy; Vukasin Ormanovic/EyeEm; Jose Luis Pelaez Inc/DigitalVision; dblight/iStock/Getty Images Plus; Nick David/DigitalVision; Peter Dazeley/Photodisc; JGI; Juana Mari Moya/Moment; Anna Erastova/iStock/Getty Images Plus; Kolopach/iStock/Getty Images Plus; Tatyana Vladimirova/iStock/Getty Images Plus; **U7:** bikec/E+; 1001slide/E+; Lysandra Cook/Moment; mallardg500/Moment; Kyrin Geisser/EyeEm; by wildestanimal/Moment; Mike Hill/Stone; Don White/E+; John W Banagan/Photodisc; James Warwick/The Image Bank; Andrea Edwards/EyeEm; Kathrin Raedel/EyeEm; Brian Mckay Photographyy/Moment; Bruno Guerreiro/Moment; dottedhippo/iStock/Getty Images Plus; Paul Starosta/Stone; Somedaygood/iStock/Getty Images Plus; R. Andrew Odum/Photodisc; cinoby/E+; vectorwin/iStock/Getty Images Plus; hakule/E+; Dorling Kindersley; hakule/iStock/Getty Images Plus; Anna Erastova/iStock/Getty Images Plus; **U8:** Christine Müller/EyeEm; wiratgasem/Moment; Mint Images/Mint Images RF; clubfoto/iStock/Getty Images Plus; Alexandra Lorenz/iStock/Getty Images Plus; Santiaga/iStock/Getty Images Plus; Piotr Marcinski/EyeEm; lenazap/E+; Westend61; Yutthana Chumkhot/EyeEm; Ultima_Gaina/iStock Editorial; tatyana_tomsickova/iStock/Getty Images Plus; Lane Oatey/Blue Jean Images; Jupiterimages/Stockbyte; Nerthuz/iStock/Getty Images Plus; Avalon/Universal Images Group; Yevgen Romanenko/Moment; milanfoto/iStock/Getty Images Plus; Preto_perola/iStock/Getty Images Plus; Mutlu Kurtbas/E+; Tomekbudujedomek/Moment; macroworld/E+; Sohel Parvez Haque/EyeEm; Jeffrey Coolidge/Stone; tatyana_tomsickova/iStock/Getty Images Plus; Lane Oatey/Blue Jean Images; Anna Erastova/iStock/Getty Images Plus; Kolopach/iStock/Getty Images Plus; kostenkodesign/iStock/Getty Images Plus; **V01:** Drazen_/E+; PeopleImages/iStock/Getty Images Plus; kirin_photo/iStock/Getty Images Plus; Mix and Match Studio/500px; **V02:** izusek/E+; MachineHeadz/iStock/Getty Images Plus; Jupiterimages/Goodshoot; **V03:** kilukilu/iStock/Getty Images Plus; Imgorthand/E+; Nick Dolding/Photodisc; Kittkavin Kao Ien/EyeEm; Jake Wyman/The Image Bank; **V04:** Kasipat Phonlamai/EyeEm; marugod83/iStock/Getty Images Plus; SelectStock/Vetta; **EMT:** Anna Erastova/iStock/Getty Images Plus; 8213erika/iStock/Getty Images Plus; Picnote/iStock/Getty Images Plus.

The following photos are sourced from other libraries.

U1: Art Heritage/Alamy Stock Photo; **U6:** ELOY ALONSO/REUTERS/Alamy Stock Photo; **V01:** Yuganov Konstantin/Shutterstock; **V04:** Air Images/Shutterstock.

Commissioned photography by Copy cat and Trevor Clifford Photography.

Illustrations

Blooberry Design; Scott Brown (The Bright Agency); Antonio Cuesta (Direct artist); Diego Diaz (Beehive); Carol Herring (The Bright Agency); Marek Jagucki (Direct artist); Michael McCabe (Beehive); Pronk Media Inc; Leo Trinidad (The Bright Agency).

Cover Illustration by Pronk Media Inc.

Audio

Audio production by Creative Listening.

Video

Video acknowledgements are in the Teacher Resources on Cambridge One

Design and typeset

Blooberry Design

Additional authors

Katy Kelly: Lock's Sounds and Spelling.

Rebecca Legros: CLIL.

Montse Watkin: Exam folder.

Freelance editor

Emma Ramirez